Also by Claire Harris

The Conception of Winter
Fables from the Women's Quarters
Travelling to Find A Remedy
Translation into Fiction
Drawing Down a Daughter

CLAIRE HARRIS

dipped in shadow

GOOSE LANE

Published by Goose Lane Editions with the assistance of the Department of Canadian Heritage and the Canada Council, 1996.

Some of these poems have appeared or will appear in *Arc, Canadian Poetry Review, Callaloo* (USA).

The author wishes to thank the Canada Council for the grant which made this book possible; and John McDowell and Robert Hilles for their stringent readings.

Edited by Laurel Boone.
Book design by Julie Scriver.
Cover photography by Dale McBride.
Printed in Canada by Imprimerie Gagné.
  10 9 8 7 6 5 4 3 2

Canadian Cataloguing in Publication Data
Harris, Claire, 1937-
  Dipped in shadow

  Poems.
  ISBN 0-86492-186-1

I. Title.
PS8565.A64825D56 1996   C811'.54   C96-950025-4
PR9199.3.H37D56 1996

Goose Lane Editions
469 King Street
Fredericton, NB
CANADA   E3B 1E5

CONTENTS

O WHAT ARE YOU THINKING   MY SISTERS
7

NUDE IN AN ARMCHAIR
13

THIS FIERCE BODY
33

SISTER   (Y)OUR MANCHILD
AT THE CLOSE OF THE CENTURY
51

WOEMAN   WOMB PRISONED
63

For John and Lyn McDowell

O WHAT ARE YOU THINKING   MY SISTERS

dear friends while you say what you're
saying in our circles   and rings   each sister
strong sister cloistered in her story
clothed in her skin

O what are you grinding black sister
black sister   what are you grinding in
your bright night skin   when I
insist on my seeing
            do you call *traitor*
                  cut eyes at me   whisper
do you   O do you   kind sister
dear friend?

what are you hatching my sister   dear
sister   what are you
hatching in your milk and cream
skin   now that glass has glittered
on Yonge and Spadina   when you see our
black brother
            do you draw your skirt closer
            cross at the corner?
my sister   my friend?

O what are you weaving dear sister
my sister   what are you weaving in
your cinnamon skin   when you read of various sons
white brothers in pedophilia   our daughters

do you fade to dream Asia   away
from your sistersm   wear caste as armour
do you vanish my friend?   O

here we dance what we're dancing in our circles   our rings
here we reach   how we reach for the moon with our teeth

And what are you rendering my sister
tender sister   what are you rendering
in your bisque China skin when
at late bus stops   a man shouts *black*
cunt
do you edge away   up stream
grumbling in the gleam away from
your sister   kind sister   dear friend?

And you forest sister   plains sister
what haunts you in your sun wheat skin
when I cry out for space   for air
dear sister   do you measure your history
first tenant   brisk friend?   O

what are you thinking far sister   far
sister to what are you listening in northern
lights skin   I read of your songs   your owls
ghost mothers from south across tundra
I reach calm sister   do I cross
your mind ever   dear sister   my friend?

here we say what we're saying in our circles   our rings
here we shine   how we shine the sun with our tongues

O what are we dreaming my sisters strong sisters
what   while we skim on the slide
of our skins   the bones of our thought
have been curved by our cultures
our flesh hung like curtains my sisters
dear friends
          and we change like the continents
(what ever our sayings our rings and our dances
how ever we tug at the sky with our eyes)
          slow
                    inexorable
scattered
                    and hiding
               deep   O our skins

NUDE IN AN ARMCHAIR

on the first saturday of every month   nO
                              matter what is/or hoar frost   nestings
                              scent of lilacs   rain   sky bled white
                                                        sky bruised
                                                        shedding

on the first saturday of every month   at
                                              eight O'clock

the girl is yOurs
the boy is yOurs

that first night my daughter shines
down to the basement
dancing for dad   the mayor
his friends   our son playing
the flute   excited
footsteps clatter   high voices proud
laughing i say sh! break a leg!
their shimmering . . .

yOur friends   bottles of rye
cameras in place

                                        downstairs low
                              growls   scattered laughter
                              shouts   men clubbing
                              jubilant below sealed doors
                                       in darkness be
                              yond firelight   perimeters

no matter what
season   the girl
the boy

yOurs

                                    upstairs   on the edge   i keep
                                    house on an acreage
                                    creeping toward abandoned
                              prairie   grasses waist high   yellow
                              mustard flogs bright stalks   bearded
                                    oats   the blasted rock
                              young under blue blue skies

                    i think we are all the best things
                    commonplace   simple   so we
                    played there slithering up on gopher
            holes to smash the young   unwary   hot &
                    laughing on on to the grey broken
                              house hollow despite
                    empire table chairs leaning in slashed
                    conversion   rosebuds straining from
                        the stalk   ghosts of windbreak
                poplars   & there you played the fiddle
                        threw sharp stones till
                                  i danced

yOurs

when the house next door burnt down
we stood like family
in the roar and bitter air
your hand on the girl's
shoulder   my arm around the boy
you said finally privacy startled i
turned to look   your eyes holes
where something leapt writhed
      boy so still

       girl rigid
i turned back to the fire   understood
i had seen flames
reflected
on the first saturday of every month   the girl
is eleven   the boy
is nine

slowly
slowly down stairs
the boy in white   & flute
the girl in pink tutu &
slippers   i remember so much
what they feared   what they dreamt:
the boy a bat carved into his hair
a red bicycle   a real easel
for the girl and one long
jangling earring
hand-in-hand they
drift to the first landing
below picasso's
dancers they turn
look up at
me

how beautiful they are   i fear the world

some nights the boy gleams
for a moment   then falls into shadow
the girl is always in half
light her profile rusty   an artifact
newly unburied   their thin backs
winged   reluctant bodies foreshortened
when they look up their eyes
are caves   in the dream i lean over
banisters   in the dream i am falling toward
i am saying   go on
i am saying   you'll be all right
in the dream i am saying   make your dad
proud   i am falling through   in the dream i
wave shoo shoo   go   go on
go on in the dream   i always wake up

yOurs
you deposit them on the bed   you
put five dollars
under the pillow
you say   she sure can dance
i say   this is too late   troubled as
if by memory   i say they're exhausted

you say its only the first saturday of every month
yOurs

minutes or months later
mama   i'm tucking in a corner   mama i
want to stop . . .
ballet   neck straightened
her face
lifted to the ceiling
like a platter

                                    i say the kids want to stop
                              you turn   their lessons   your eyes
                    flare   the air is begging my body hovers
                              over your buckle the belt circles
                        that room knuckles dance a two-step around
                              me light alive with thwacking air
                    burns your brown shoes scarred like my father's
                              someone cries   cries the ceiling swings
                              open in the mirror corners scream
                              the door snakes through air i am
                        on my knees head covered by my arms
                                          walls sob   sob

INTERIOR: COURTROOM   DAY

Judge, lawyers, witnesses, jury, court officials.
The children sit together. On either side of them
a social worker. They are wards of the court.
There are no spectators   i am grateful

the room
muffles
your
secrets burn
naked
i didn't know
floors hover
the air
is a dead
zone my
father's faces
are bear
traps faces
swing crazily
towards me
ceilings
pulse   flow
prosecutor's face
a funnel
chandeliers
ping small hail

Q:
You are under oath. Surely at that
point you knew that something was
terribly wrong?

A:
it was not the first time i had been
beaten

Q:
You expect us to believe that your
husband would beat you simply for
saying that your children no longer
wished to take ballet/to play the
flute?

A:
yes

Q:
I put it to you that you enjoyed
those beatings. That you were a
willing participant . . .

courtswells
shimmer
discordant
a nutcracker
seizes
how could i
know
the judge's
webbed wings
cling
to my hair
frozen
i
lungs stuffed
accusation
drips down
window panes
walls twist
the chair
dissolves under
faces flap

pitching off
bins in the
barn my
mother's faces
spring at
me
i didn't know
nobody
told me
nobody you women
i am dead
centre
i am in
you women who
now live
who stare
your daughters
mark me
without care
at ease now
quake
be terrified
you women
tremble
your happy homes
tremble
see clearly
your eyes
whirlpools i
swirl drown

A:
no! no!

Q:
What happened the next day?

A:
i did what women do

Q:
Why didn't you leave him? Take the
kids . . .

A:
i got up to prepare supper   when he
came in we sat down to eat . . .

Q:
Answer the question!

A:
where could i go that he couldn't
find me? how would we live? i
phoned the police they said no lock
could keep a man out   would they
be better off if i were dead?

Q:
You said yourself you could not
protect them!

over benches
tectonic
plates shift
in cracks a type
writer plays
tchaikovsky
my mothers spin
past windows
the jury
the flute
dances past
my lips
rest on the box
without care
for the moment
i am dead
you burn
vultures
fly from your
mouths
flap
in court-air
wings
brushing
against
i am a cliff
i am
granite
i live even
with your nests

your polar
eyes
the liar speaks
sweetly
the devil does
not stammer
he smiles & smiles
and listens
and speaks of love
and listens
the creak in
the heart   O
the thirst in
the heart
you women   your
grim teeth
yOur daughters
yOur babies
O

A:
i wanted to live . . . i tired
. . . hurt.

Q:
You have testified that you lied on
the two occasions that you went to
the hospital . . .

A:
i was ashamed . . . i thought every
wo . . .

Q:
Your pride wouldn't allow you to
protect yourself, or your children.
Do you consider yourself a fit mother?

A:
i didn't know what was happening
to the children   i didn't know

on my ledges
my breasts
no
longer ache
my mouth
is a crack
i am
white cliffs
my voice:
small stones
you women
O
your daughters
will mourn
will tremble
will dissolve
yOur daughters
yOur babies
O

my eyes beg   the children
become stone

23

yOurs

light years ago
you are a bolt in the sky
we   like any picasso woman   are plane
move in segments   disjointed
our limbs never where we left them
our eyes   wombs   and you are molten brass
volcanic
you swallow the world:
look   these are hands of
a man who works hard for his family
a man who protects
                              light years ago
we shrivel   girl
is a wound   boy
ash

on the first saturday of every month
                              at eight O'clock
in the locked
basement
        girl   is yOurs
        boy   is yOurs

                              brown stains on her pants
                                      she is hesitant
                                   i take her in my arms
                      this is what it means to be a woman
                         she is a woman now a woman   i
                         rock her a woman i rock and rock
                              now   woe woe woeman

i say   she is
i say she is woman now
too old to dance

relief draws its map
into your face   never
never too old to dance for papa
he puts his arm around her
she is bone
she is line
he kisses   loudly
laughs dances her
pats her bottom   slips
her twenty dollars
it flutters to the floor

it is then i know

she is an absence
i remember

on the first saturday of every month

                                        at eight
                    mirrors gleaming   mums in the window
                        house a beacon on the edge   i host
                            a card party   wives of all your
                    friends   later the doctor   the minister's
                            wife   it was a test
                            how could anyone believe

in the basement   the girl
danced in her slippers
wooden zest on
her face   herself
curled tight
in her own womb   hiding
from the lascivious
gleam of their husbands   while
in the corner   a nude
boy played the flute

on the first saturday of every month   you
auctioned yOur tender
flesh

                                              i am no longer
                             mama no no   nor mummy
                                     no!   and beneath
                            such wrappings there is
                                 fine strong muscle
                               i am a shelled thing
                   eaten   left is the husk   white
                                        calcareous

                                        i am all there is

in their small
throats   i
no longer a call
a note

on the first saturday of every month
the procedures are simple   dignified
greetings   conversation   tchaikovsky
a wine punch in silver wedding bowls
hors d'oeuvres   we wait on sylvie my
throat taut   our mayor's wife always
late if she doesn't come i will know if
she doesn't come   the world ended
meanwhile   there are fresh blossoms
on the table   meanwhile varied linen

wild rose china cut glass shimmering i
wait   white curdle of hope/no/hope she
comes chattering   garnished with pearls
and the night is not rags not flaming
despite the girl palely pink and delicate
curves   boy in white & flute   no
dogs howl   air comes back in cat's yawn
in the whispering of cards   the even
rhythm of cakes and coffee   i am not jael
i do not take hammer   or nail   down
stairs they divide the spoils   to each
in turn the girl   the boy
on the first saturday of every month   nO
                                                              matter what season
                                                                the girl   thirteen
                                                                the boy   eleven

uh   um   the girl stares through the open
window   in the scent of dust and hedges   um
I haven't had a period

                                                       hands clench the dough
                                                    it swells through my fingers

for three months

                                    bees in the lilacs
                        for this moment was i born
                  for this moment my mother's silence
                    the handyman's fingers   her rage
                        my father's clogging games
                        for this moment   this girl
                    who never mouthed a refusal

but she flops into a chair her limbs tubes
her breasts thrusting against
her legs crossed at the ankle   she is still
open and apart   waiting a man's gaze   a nude
with a belly like an orange
at fourteen   a watchful teasing
malevolence   sketched threat in the shadows   i saw
your friend
the doctor   she wants to see
you   tomorrow
it can't wait till the first saturday

                                          i breathe in
                        does she want to see your father

no . . . just my mother

she stares and stares

cabbage whites dance in the arbor

                                        i will not split
                            along seams   i wait

the door bangs shut

                        now seventeen months later I stand
                    on the rim of this new city   the woman
                    here scribbling   bright black   in my
                new house   white walls white carpet white
                            sofas clutch at pale prairie sky
                    at unconcerned gusts   she holds out
                    a black hand   sprays of white gladioli
                    whisper   a poem is distraction   wild
                    comfort   we need more than poems
                prayers   she expects nods   agreement
                dressed all in white I reach for the flute
            (a dirge fades to the window/tumbles slowly down
                    roofs/river/banks slips from trees/slides
                        on a thin rime of ice) I might if I
                    weren't so tired   but she drifts away
                something ragged awkward flung like a trap
                to pavement draws the red honda   Adam
            in denim jacket   jeans   neon-yellow sweater
                waves at me   I lean on air   carved white

victorian sills watch   wait   Julie   her
beautiful hair chopped into purple green
pink quills   white coat flapping open on
brown sweater   tight jeans   strides the walk
gleaming metal belt clanging as she moves
she does not look up   I hear a knock
pounding   shrill calls   a white seething
of breakers boils around rock   I find
a smile . . . I have not practised my L . . .

THIS FIERCE BODY

                        despite
this fierce body

i arrive without weapons
your call sudden   without pity

something has happened to the air

you say *i am* . . . gesture vaguely
pluck at the bedsheets . . . *AIDS*
air scalded
you say *keep my secret*

as if no one had spoken

the word   homeless

your room dips into shadow

now your fevered faces gleam against faded
pillows   electronic IV a mast where courage/
anguish billow giant sails
women   we sit isolated   chairs window other
bed   gasping on your beach   all air
gone into those sails
seconds minutes wash over   rock
us where we sit   you swim away floundering
just beyond fingertips
closet doors gape   philosophical mums wilt
above your head tulips dim
what is there to attempt   except
the banal   talk all gossip and olympiad

in truth
no riddles interest you   except one
you watch   eyes wicked/delighted   when two others
burst in hands full   wide Cochrane sky
caught in early crocus   you rise to a frisson
of hysteria   we plunge blooms
into jugs   glasses   a bottle   you
thank us   you smile
as into a mirror   in your too blue eyes
crocus droop
your thirty-five-year-old flesh melts   burning
you go before   a man fierce   enarmoured
of cynicism and faith

who would not weep

friend something of you diminished
yet escaping these marks
trails through air   like smoke
face it
the whole damn episode yourself
life/death   constructed
with the same reckless ferocity
others construct
an athlete
see here the bones:
you are born   house warm
comfortable   full of laughter
you are three   God
raises his eyes   your father
dies   mother's little man
an altar boy
charmed by precision
pageantry
clean cut of church law
between altar
and rails
you give yourself
wholeheartedly
at fifteen you know
who you are

by inches
joy curdles   and love
the word becomes thrust
wit   bitter   edged
as you fought through clouds
of gall
self bruised
east-end contempt
of/for women
inherited
turned now against you
male   blessed
in the arms of males
between this   and your Catholic
desire for absolutes
there was no place
in your philosophy
for you
you learn to dissemble
a second self   restless
you become a teacher
try abstinence
restless
you fall in love
you try commitment
restless
you enter a seminary

nothing works   you return to gut
loneliness   six months   restless
you begin to cruise
searching night streets
retreat
confession
penitence
restless
daily mass at Sacred Heart
restless
the streets again
mass again
absolution
and so
and thus
and how
on to the last lover
your skin erupts
Vancouver? San Francisco?
Calgary?
now you cruise clubs
listening everywhere
for the skeleton
with jester's bells
mass again
and lies
you hold your secret

only now and again
a volcanic bitterness
a spitting in the face
of fate
hating your skin
a reckless driving
restless
to be rid
and mass again . . .

in the face of this   what
consolation
when your doctor   eyes shivering behind
his brightness   opens the door
we slip out   hastily discard imaginary
masks   our whispered *see you wednesdays*
rush to greet gulping breaths
where Calgary streams through the grasp
of a chinook and brown grass
gleams in soft winter light

today you stride the room   stretch   swing your arms
cheeks flushed   determined   how well
you wear rumpled hospital blue   checked
blue edged robe   elegant
as bone   vivid in your dying
alone with you i do not ask
your face a rosetta stone   i remember
our grievous assurance in a religion class
i'm saying   *it's the most important thing you'll*
ever do   dying you say to all that crowded life
pray you're conscious   you wouldn't
want to miss it
what now you've come to it so soon

i cannot hear the flutter of wings   anywhere

from your window we watch mist and february steep
the river banks   among ghost poplars athletes run eloquent
this loneness of cats   one paces the swift
Bow in its narrow channel   a woman surrounded by
herself   morning miles always boring until the machine takes
over and she escapes her fierce body

you watch with the intensity of one who hears for
the first time the body's silent hum   sees creamy
ball and socket   pull and taut of muscles   slosh/
flow/rumble   pink/lilac/blue insides   like planets
the banks are crowded with office joggers   hazards
dog   ice   she wouldn't know   we are amazed at this
luxury   lost ones climb from nests under the crossing
dead wave from hospital windows   she wouldn't
see   to win one must be furious   monkish in pursuit
crosswalk glows red   she runs wind blows chill she
runs   can't stop won't stop for years   you say *God
i hear stone upon stone   i hear eyes turn in sockets*
while this lust takes her your bruised finger points
she is so powerfully alive and glimmering   clear on
her threshold   like you in your dying

from a great height you say *I'm going*
to unplug this   remove these tubes
there's no hope

no etiquette for such a moment
no syntax   we are left
with ourselves
and closeted

when
soon
does anyone else know
no
call home first
she'll try to change my mind
you must
why
your death   not yours alone

bruised eyes crinkle gleam
but you say nothing

talked to anyone
my priest
we struggle up this corridor   turn left
into dimness   re-enter your room
it's so hard
i take your arm

we are speaking not at all   or in hushed whispers   you lie
curled   manchild no longer held to the breast of death but
death itself   and your bed rises around you   where you are
everything is metaphor   flowers that won't last   this illness
that thrives on meaning   a dim graveyard wind   your chest
heaves where you stroke out   stroke out (in the hall loud
noises   running footsteps   a voice   a door slams) the plastic
manacle slides on your wrist   hands huge   erupting skin
stretched red tight clasped between your knees   sweat
gathers in hollows   your beard grows your nails   here is
rot   you want us to leave   to stroke your eyelids to leave
we know   but we cannot again abandon you to plague and
grim waters   shadows jeer from banks   whispers run long
shoals/ vicious rocks jut   *in extremis*   in extreme unction   on
the scent of holy oils   rise and fall   *de profundis*   whispered
aves   inhaling the scent of beeswax incense we dream you
grace and light   fruit   and scented gardens   the long ease
knowing you stand accused   but believing here is the print
without the foot   guilt without sin

you wake suddenly blush say apropos of nothing perhaps *i am
going home* so it is every cliché we have ever read

44

i know that dying is another way
of seeing
you've shared everything else
and you're the first person
i've seen die
i want to know   really
but i'm afraid you'll tell me
insisting on my presence   beyond
i'm so tired
the light seized by cheering hills
i'm failing you say
                    delicately
waving

now
death is become AIDS   destroyer of worlds

now
our every gesture   a conspiracy with the grave

for a day
and a half your face seems luminous
then bone begins to seep through skin
it should take a week your doctors say
five and a half days
while you starve
                              hesitate
                teeter

now
gravedusk coiling   coiling through your gut

each day
that is left   a long grey burden   weight of a life
pressing you down   every morning born old

now
the room strained to your tiniest whisper

that week

full of third page headlines   small rumours of plague   war
godwrath: Genesis of Plague Deaths Lack of Money Vaccines
No Use Condoms Biblical Condemnations Test Proposals Drugs
Users Source of Infection Isolation Suggestions Gloves for
Police Forces Lack of Research Firings School Pickets Gays
March Promiscuity Heterosexual Population Threatened Blood
Transfusions Infected Gay Man Charged With Spreading Virus
in Tears Babies Born Wonder Drug in Mexico Wonder Drug in
Paris Wonder Drug in The Bahamas at home Advertisements
To Be Reviewed Too Explicit Truth Not in Interest of Population
Law of Internment As Public Danger Passed MLAs' Raises
Pass Lack of Interest Lack of Money   no lack of hellfire/fear

third day
like a man dismantling a roof tile by tile   you work
carefully   already our faces wither

fourth day
or like a skater   slow deliberate each long stroke
towards that horizon where sons fall blazing   angels
to whatever waits   we joke   whisper   you teach us
Moonlight Sonata over and over again   we are salvaged
from sentimentality

fifth day
there is no flesh left to lose   you stir   toss   kick off
blankets too hot   too cold   air too heavy   traffic loud
the Bow blinding   your dying becomes this long dispute
with life argued in miasma of incontinence   of disinfectant
of heroin   and a sister's powerful binding love

sixth day
shadow on the lip of the grave   we slip from the room
to walk in air   to count days   remember . . .
just one more day to be borne   towards evening   increase
the dosage! but we can't he might overd . . .
this is not a marathon!   your skin bubbles   melts
we shatter   a jigsaw   hold on   put ourselves together
hiding the awkward angles   shading our pain into yours

long ago   i
thought   crudely
you would become
thread
down which one might
climb
to peer into depths
eyes
adjusted through you
see all   then
back
to riverwind
              skychatter

SISTER   (Y)OUR MANCHILD
           AT THE CLOSE OF THE
           TWENTIETH CENTURY

Dream warrior   day after day   my sister watches
him haunt weathered grass his face defines time
into sight   stalk   still   kill   his small body
stippled with shadowy leaf with stem   crouched
down into maleness   her *beautiful man who kills*
Cat explodes over the stream to the neighbour's
yard not dead though he leaps bang bang pudgy legs
finding the death stamp   his face radiant   she
watches him   day after day   carving away chunks of
soul of tenderness empathy awe   each day more
hollow   each day after cops-an-criminals   after
settlers-an-indians   stones like teeth   WARS ON
DRUGS WARS ON CRIME WARS ON DRUNK DRIVERS
WARS   after the unread books   the screen's
fraudulent epiphanies   after hours staring down the
mirror dreaming his future in its skinny arms   after
a musty locker room stalking   the girl who cd/wd
who deserved it   suddenly he is 18 swallowed by
that image where exultant cameras linger caress
lightning smiles   O thunderclaps in high fives
golden warriors drunk on the death
                              of *cockroaches/ sand*
                                        niggers
                         in that other garden
                              old Eden   Iraq

          time's a rubber band

a bottomless well my sister
watches
as if she'd never
love again   she watches
            Sister's son leaves
leaves his moist
childhood   (as if he did not
know he'd
run upstairs   was
lodged
in her heart)
goes from her quiet
warmth   her sly jests
his place
in her voice   he
goes from her   from
my sister
as if he had no past

                eager   he goes to the marines
                to the running   foul grunting
                sweet guns to stalking hunting
                killing   to old savage pieties
                slicked into smoothness
                            his cap tossed
                to presidential air

in *Harper's Magazine* John Lukacs writes that the essence of
revolutionary movements sputtering in the oddest places of
the so-called Third World was a tribal hatred of foreign, in most
cases, white power. That this kind of hatred was, in most
instances, as unjustified as it was short sighted is another matter.

massive this blindness
to the human heart   such poverty
puffs the will
to commodify even dignity
signalling like
dead grain elevators on the prairie
a small town   narrowed
to hamlet

in such a mind
the world glimpsed through the wavering aura of migraine five/ten
million Africans trapped branded transported twice five/ten dying
in the attempt the three hundred years of slavery rape its terrible
aftermath otherness fear and police boots batons bullets joblessness
fear invisibility the ceaseless niagaras of difficulty that idiot's tape
measure fear   we who have as wings only hope   only the feather's
bruising courage to make it come out even
a small thing
a footnote of history
in such a mind
the depopulation of vivid teeming Americas brown people wrenched
from the circle to vacancy the land despoiled   bewildered wo/men
Alcohol Lakes   children Davis Inlets   bereft ancestors   mountains
in such eyes
death   bone-white and richly dressed in silks
sits down to feast on the dark   the innocent mountains of dark
dead the growing mountains of dead   without tenderness   in such
a mind a small thing
mere detail to evoke
                    the historian's nostalgia
                    prick the midget soul

Were the Turks still in charge of Mesopotamia, were the Spanish of Cuba, the British of India, wouldn't we be better off? And wouldn't their subject peoples be better off?

                              my sisters   the white man's
                                      burden is still borne
                                         on the backs of
                                       Africans   Asians
                                    Aboriginal peoples
                                    Women   children
                    the bearing enforced by fists and bombs

                in such a mind
                subjugation is a gift

in such a mind
the mutilation of peoples   planet   skies
in such a mind
AIDS?   (Atlanta: culture of vaccine in monkey's blood to be tested
in Central Africa?)   the cigarette's cancer   chemical abuse and
shifted nuclear wastes   new greeds   dead Romany Jews Palestinians
in such a mind   lost graces   decencies   knowledge   bled
resources the common humanity shattered into us and them
the curved ribs of starvelings
a small thing
in such a mind
a very small thing

                my sisters watch
                      we are not
                  or   even safe

                    my sisters   we must watch
                                even with our own young
                    we are not

                    the world we
                            helped birth

the boy does not read Lukacs   he does not need to
his is a simple   savagery   he makes the world safe
for exploitation by Europe North America whoever
else the floundering raft may hold
                                my sister watches
a flailing president
his tantrum   his
            e
        v nomous
                    autumn
                            slither
                        through
                            the
                    world
                rear
            into
        hot
        blood
            graves
                shed
                    skin
                    coil
                in
                to
        win
            ter

life   a coffle of wrenching questions
this poem   only
  stilled
life

and certain
skies alive with random bombers

my sister   Somalia is a vague memory   a hot day in grade school
Jim sticking a girl's damp braid to his desk with chewing gum
now you inhale this news   you pull out the atlas   now you wait
on the small screen murderous men   men without
      mothers
Sister   your house
      trembles
(y)our boy calls   the air shudders   morning dissolves   a sudden
dusk droops in the garden   slides over mourning dishes   fills
the kitchen sink   floats a miasma over office chat   ghosts in
computer screen   drips grey-green from noon trees   by five
your small house itches with sadness drenched in dusk   death
Sister   your nights will be a broken watching   you will walk
in fog till he comes home   earless you watch   and walk in this
already your neck curves back your mouth strains against time
you fumble for the moment of his turning   his
exultation/exaltation flash
                    flashing through the line

Iraq . . . Panama . . . Grenada . . . Somalia . . . Bosnia
what's the diff 'long as it's not here
'long as   beyond their reach
we can do it from the air

                              life is blood   we   who
                              are civilized   dread
                              the smell of blood
                              still   from a distance
                              our bombs
                              are poets
                              O   my sisters
                              think of *Guernica*

              Sister   I say it though saying it is terror
              we suffer the ignorance of those never bombed   those
              never poor   we suffer those who lack imagination
              we suffer greed and more   we suffer race war
              we who midwife evil call it realism

an Iraqi sister rages back at our screens
you think we are Red Indians? you can not
come here and kill us we are human too I have
forgotten the date   I have forgotten your
face   my sister   I have forgot every thing
except these words we gave you (this was
on CNN so must be true)   her scattered
house behind her crouched hours stench and
dead babies   grim water   warrior sons   my
sisters behind her scalped Blackfoot   Crow
their raped tortured women   and the babies'
brains   pinkish grey moss on virgin pines
behind her   my mothers   my little sisters
chained above deck   divided
                              from brothers fathers
              earth

(a) pleasure of those captains
tools of gentlemen owners
            of a new minted
      Canadian
                  saint

            on still green earth
            the scorpion panics
      hibiscus bleeds red petals
            lilac stiffens   dies
      the Bow slides softly
                  beneath

            the cobra
twists mingles with a stone bush

                  Sister   a chinook gentled
                        warm in my palm   here
                        take it
                  they say soft winds heal

he flies away your baby boy man flies away   you remember Croatian
mountain roads winding through broken babies Bosnia   full horror
of rape as policy   at least not that (your fingers sprout tubers
            only Somalia surely there   (your face slides
                  wide smiles
surely there the expected bent vulnerability

now the first American marines to set foot in Africa   they land
trapped by Hollywood   by their own bloody history   dazzled by four
centuries of lies   by CNN lights cameras action
      in this polluted gaze
                        Africa
      meets my sister's son

Africa
         and he has never seen flamingos
rise   a brisk whispering cloud
     splashing across scudding skies

     and he has never seen in happy chatter
   kohled eyes over market tables   bleached
          earth yards their round gossiping houses
     full carved doors   bursting
                      granaries
     kindness

Africa
          that various surprising complexity that black
        wine   sure as the hour before dawn
     its pressed suited civil servants pouring from fever-haunted
   huts onto wide boulevards   green with spirits of ancestors
     and bone-rhythms   nor has he seen the red blossoming stumps
                      of children   their playgrounds/
          corn fields/foot paths seeded with our mines
               nor has he heard griots sing its old "primitive"
   rejection of total war or seen such grace such ancient majesty
               not even the skull in its smile
       its sun-dried elders   baobabs   vast bright silences
          river lives   phut-phuts   skyscrapers
          even its frequent original hells are a surprise

to Africa he goes with his good Canadian buddies our Airborne
he goes   as one who goes
                      on safari
there he is sent   Lance Corporal Kelly
to guard the street outside the hotel

there most foreign reporters live
in Mogadishu   my sisters   frustrated
he speaks to the *Manchester Guardian's*
John Lancaster   he speaks for attribution
I think every marine came here with the idea that he might get
a chance for a confirmed kill

O my sisters
it is past midnight   at her moon table our sister sits
her face a geometry of angles   une de Les Demoiselles
                              serpent fingers
          hover furtive
                         anonymous clippings
                  their poisonous envelopes

          white horses fly the ceilings   their five
hundred year wings muscular beat death death
death   outside her window snow
does not drift upwards   below the ragged forsythia
the stream is not stilled

WOEMAN   WOMB PRISONED

A
  b
CHILD BIRTH
    e   l
    s   e
    s   s
      i   s
        n   i
        g   n
            g

or
          s   n
              i

we tell   ourselves
our younger selves
dancing to the three musicians
                              sterilized
beyond
mangled hours   furious panic
we tell ourselves   roofing
our huts
                        as in midnight movies
we tell   ourselves
our little sisters
beyond
each breath   fished
from desperate waters
                          & triumphant
we tell ourselves
turning away with/out tears

                              i

              I   *n*

          n

KNOTTED LIVE

          t   *r*   *r*

      r   *i*   *r*

  i   *c*   *o*

      c   *a*   *r*

  a   *t*

  t   *e*

e   *r*

  r

woman   torn silk   wyman
sunrise of burst mango
uman uncertain
stone peeping between   & who
owman
a nourishing darkness
whoman   only
a weel
(wicker trap catching his fish
wyfman owing windsucker
welcome
his winder to wield
woeman wimbled   her waul

why   and hammered into moon

woman   womb-prisoned
forever and ever we follow rabbit
down the dark hole

65

a blessing
we tell ourselves
our little birds

            now
look here at her   fleshed
word:

fifteen   & committing
birth alone   nine
months ridden down to
silence

                         (consider
what if
      dreaming you
      were trapped in rock
what if
      there a cruel
      collar hung
      about the neck
what if
      you swallowed it
what if
      you woke   choking
      found your belly
      hard   high   and stone
         moving . . .

now
and now
knowing she lies awake where
now is knowledge is not lucid

(for Jenn   something requiring a new
choreography   how to move   breathe
see)   for us

                                        still without volition
                        though some know the landmarks
                                        still helplessly alive
                        before the womb   and its fragile
                        flickering wicks in puffs of flesh
                                        still wedged tight
                                        under boards
                                        under crushing
                                                        law
                                church
                        custom
boulders (eighth century   forested european north boychild tree-cradled
pork in his mouth   gold   silver talisman   that who travelled his path
would know he was loved   and noble)
        bondage

                dans montréal (1784)   une esclave   noire
breeder   (mare to be ridden   mer to drown in   mère
        waits comforting
                        confronting
        this dark reality
                kisses tiny brown toe/pink sole/palm
                                strokes curved lip
                between   this softness   her
life fold into lifefold life
        into fold noire de la petite

under recessed rods of daylight
Room shifts   licks a fingertip
turns the page   downstairs hall
clock strikes midnight   Room
trailing dry whispers across

terror
her blind alley (ally)

the child in her shunts towards light

no one knows   no one will   ever   not her Father not her brother
no teacher snobby kids   no neighbours   she hugs Boogie Bear . . .

in the beginning such pain twanged
ribs crawl   cramp at her tummy   she
leans into the atlas her nails dig at its
battered covers   lips clamp shut after
in pale sweat she pulls down the long
loose sweater bulky cardigan slides from
her desk   before giggling cruel stares
in the girls' washroom she bolts into a
cubicle   sinks in to think if there is
time   her Father's hard   "real ill   call
me"   He mustn't know   if *it* came out
here   back of a bus   she could never
go to school anywhere   it would be in
all the papers   on TV   He will kill her
He will find a way   He   afraid she'd faint
away she empties her purse   counts
twice   convinced by pain that comes
again

pauvre she

to wind her terrible strength   *to hug free*

at last

                    la belle enfant terrible

                              in/to

        thank God Almighty

                              finality

then clasps the body

        its slow stiffening

                              free

              at least

                    still centuries later   perfume   morning coffee
                    soaps news   our dread of whatever day ahead of/
                    unaware   chained   censor in/of our own history
                    "it's this disposable society   girls think they can
                    throw anything away" envious of the baby she
                    cannot bear vitriol handing in the air we tangle
                    as if for a woman this were something new   as if
                    we have not always plotted our courses   steered
                    our barques towards courage   mild revolt   secrecy
                    as if we have not always been "responsible"   all
                    bodies though unfree in our own   war in/fertility
                    pestilence rape dalliance a surfeit of daughters the
                    second coming   (woe to whoever shall be with
                              child shall give suck in those days
                                        and still woe

        why

                                        hence the Attic
                                        put out

                    throw out

69

she waits till the others have gone
one   banging at her cubicle "water
OK?"   lively false concern   sshshsh
pneumatic sigh washroom door closing
her legs spaghetti she waits   uneasy
to phone a cab   waits slumped behind
pillars   stumbles into the back seat
hides   school's taxi's indifferent eyes
just time to drop notes coins in dry
brown palm hurry past puzzle of hoar
frost hedges the front door   shut   pain
curls   her   Mummy   Oh   Mom
Mummy

sick   wobbly
she moves care/full   Room
ripe with strange weather

Lot's daughter   she
must bear in
and silence

this   long ago   still
Jenny   only
twelve and a half   ambulance kicking
small stones   as she turns the corner
begins to run   Mom Momeee she chases   Momeee
after it past her house faster faster
stitch in her side   faster   red siren
speeds away   o world   o
                        hollow light
that hath such things in it

exposed in earthenware
       found lying on the ground

                    hence the Latin
                       toss out
                offered

       all these of a babe
       exposed outside the home
        in a public place
        without a name though
        garments marked
        tokens of love hidden in folds
      for rescue by one who needs
      a child or a slave

                and yet Euripides
  the best of mortals and those who are not love children

perhaps
    except under black light   *wyman*
               why then?
       consider (
       or hungry Irish) feet   blue bare
       in Toronto winter   bodies cough
       cluster before scant coal listen
       that new mouth open   by pallid
       morning it's blue as feet   flaky
       skin stretched to
              sacrifice

       the man dead snoring   his woman
        gaunt on the rocks
              of Scylla
       yes his

                her mother's return
                her mother's desperate packing
where are you going
                she sits on the bed holds her too hard
                too close
I'll send for you darling

                then as it were a debt
I had a baby in my tummy
I . . . ab . . .
it died

                                                home movies: her
                                                Father's eyes glitter
                                                His already pale face
                                                pallid   His voice grates
                                                on the whetstone
                                                deep in His throat
                                                His whisper denies
                                her a mother   Scarlet Woman!
                                                get out get out get
                                                doors bang shut
                                the yellow hall drains light
                                                alien   snakes round
                                stairs to stone-laid kitchen

The first time He came to her   tickling
she   grateful for play in the pink and white
Room   tickled back
        you
just   un(e
        just like your mother

nota bene
if he saw   he would smash at her
another fault in his earth   and
damned like her too fertile body
and he perceived not when she lay
down   *nor her rising*
in its terrible
learning

where
she is and is

WHYWHYWHYWHY WHY EVER THUS
not HOW   we know HOW   WHYANDWHYAND   WHY
as battle cry it lacks something   clarity
wyman
so bears responsibility for disarray   on
all philosophical fronts   flat or pendulous
who ever knew women to fight well   not at
their best

you

who are here   and h/ uman
imagine
her outside wor(l)ds with what
traumatic
frenzy she stands on that rock
sea sucking
at her feet drawing wet rags
about her
bruised breasts catching spume & spray
blistered

just not un(e
like
like
     your mother
          mother
     (W h O r E)
          mother

pain grabs her   hangs her
from ceilings   Room
screams   she now is
engrossed   brown sparrow   she
batters against plate glass
rags of breath hard   laboured   blanket
between braced teeth
still when He knocks on her door
"are you decent?" she is
and sore afraid till His Head withdraws
till the front door clicks
shut in her tummy

she drifts through sulky
rooms   open
like Chinese boxes sundered
through whispering fog
yellow and white butterflies
sift towards seamed horizon
red twigs in the far away
she sees her mother
who sits in a leisure of dawn   safe
where a rush of water soars
stumbling   she looks behind

                                        silence
                                 she mounts air
                        slips through to the keep where
                                    nothing is
                  sound   an absence she brushes against
                                      imagine
                          her passover into alone
                               the putting
                          herself to silence

                    which is
            that **small hammer**
                          distilled spirit
        at want of flavour
                    which is
                    suppressed
                    and she **silentiary to**
                    concealment   watches her future
        fold   a silent
            movie   now she climbs tall roofs
                                                (so

                    outside   why (high
        of community
                          outside   houses (our
            of meaning
                               inside yoke (ache
                consider her at night
            wyfman to
                in the silence
                               of ovulation
            and
                    this
                    fear   this loss

                              75

                                        knows   there is no
                                   measuring such distance

He will find a way . . . to kill her   He will beat . . . her
body shudders   erupts   words He makes her recite: *and*
the younger arose went unto her father   he perceived
not when she lay down nor when she arose   ashes stones
hot on raped tongue   shivering   hall clock bongs noon
into small bones   her face   Mummy   Mom   Oh Mummy

she drifts past her mirror   stranger glimpsed
at the end of a tunnel   framed by light

                                        her mother
                            long ago one August at harvest
                    entered the barn came surely to her stall
                        it's such hard work   your whole body
                        aches   you do it out of love   growing
                        things   she had smiled down at her
                                    you are my harvest
                                    words spill into straw
                                ping through silvered glass

her face already different   somehow

a sane early moon
creeps across the gap in her
blinds   drops
               (
)
alone as any god
too young to trust that every
thing ends   surely

man above
consider her knotted
                    remembering
                                how & long
          lifted arms   how
                                        finger once
          searched   eye brow
      curve of jaw
          how tongue came alive
                        in hollows   throat
              and how   once
  pierced by   curls
                    strength   its
white hot centre
              strand by strand
                    climbing
          through joy   to
    revelation
              braying down
              moons

  she now thins
              a skeleton   trapped in stone air
              she can scarcely recall softness
              hardened beyond wonder   beyond
              how
                    why

          (their proper
                        improper
              behaviour
                        as words

for a brief moment we imagine each other
my sky shades to midnight   hers cracks

hauled into a black hole rebellion growls
shrieks to the empty house explodes into
fuck Youuu . . . I feel I dream I want . . . You
can't just hang a life on me! words bloom
thick as summer ivy crowd the room   fear
scalds her   God The Father   Male . . . not
fair . . .

and so
          and how
                        night
        stumbles
into dawn

twenty six hours   every twenty
every fifteen
every . . .
so that she forgets
breathing
though she practised
ever since she felt those first
flutters   knew she was on her own
Lot's Daughter
and still she prays feverishly   blindly
when the punishment recedes   prays
each time   she can't help crying out
Mummy   Mom   Mummy   needing her

it stops

                    now tied
as to Parsee towers   she
            waits
                          waits centuries &
        the high wide smiles
                of vultures
                              female
            their threadbare coats
                              hats
                    cold water faces
                      their biblical
              suspicion
    (Luke 12:29): See
    lilies how they grow   toil not
    neither spin (which church father
                          in denial
        starvation fertility
        cold joblessness
        disease
                      seeing sex as uman
          not quite human
        merely an occasion
                          of sin
        thinking   burn
          in chastity
                  or shrivel
        in s(k)in   only have faith
                            wrote
    so shall your Heavenly
                Father . . . (naturally
                without consulting
                Her)

this unravelling bed
blind fears   she cannot feel *it*
perhaps nothing is happening . . .

on television a Chinese woman
hoes in paddy fields   enormous
skies streaked with sheer silken
skeins   everywhere others
work ankle deep in mud and water
but the camera isolates this woman
against a cool blue sky   her face
Serene Acceptance
stands places her right hand
on her waist   grimaces
moves slowly to where she's left a bundle
in a stand of shade trees
unrolls bright mats slowly   squats
with only a grunt
to confront   to comfort reality   after
so very few minutes   healthy
kittenish squalling on the wind
rich male voice
over   assuring her   child birth
is a natural process
in an hour this mother will be
at work   and so she is

long before the midnight show is over

it is something she has done
wrong   she doesn't know   or
pleasure   female
her fault

                    alone
          she waits
            that long
                                un
        s   e   e   *ly*
              m

                      t
              h)   *u*
                          m
                  b
                                l

              e
          into final air
                      rocks
          spewing her
                      out

          mother   murther   murder

                          whirling
              open into
                      Charybdis

never again midnight skies draw moons   or ever
lake-dreaming cities never again   hoar frost
blest trees   never pure joy dawn stars fogged
lights unlistened silence never again cop cars
their circling eye or safety never again sleep
without dream or the honest unreckoning eye of
husband of children never never never   light
or clean dark

caught in
    convers(at)ion
of folding faulting

perhaps in spite of every thing
that inside her is   and
angry   she hopes *it* is not
or hurting   imagine   kids   teachers
knowing your father
                      is
              your grandfather not
fair

                              once on television   she
                                  saw babies   bottles
                                      in a lab . . .

she must not think . . .
it is dead she knows that

in films at school the woman pushes   pushes
cries out   holds laughing arms to her child
since they make you go   least they could do
is tell the truth   liars! liars! liars!

this time she'll die
courage deserts her
Mummy   Oh Mom   please come   God
let her come . . .

                          she is kneeling on the sill   her
                              belly a great moon
                  her mother's voice rises to the window
                          Jenngirl . . . run run!

consider Therese Le Vasseur

woeman
wyfman to
> *Rousseau   tearing from her side*
> *her **fifth** infant (and did he mark*
> *its clothes to silence her cries*
> *record the marks*

> *as he had done*
> *for their **first girl** but not its*
> *birth date   his promises quarter*
> *small rooms*

> *her **second** rides frost*
> *potatoes   babbles in cabbage stew*
> *promises more sisters*

> *her **third** pressed between covers*
> *his papers his books*

> *her **fourth***
> *gusts through   cracks in his eyes*
> *her grief   shattering their poor*
> *ceilings not his repute . . . ain't*
> *a man gotta do what a man's . . .*

> *he did not "boast of it publicly*
> *solely   out of regard for their*
> *mother"   thus all his children*
> *"deposited in a foundling home"*

but there is nowhere to run
she cannot even if she tried
                    she read
this woman pushed pushed
her guts came . . . liver lights
she does not know . . .
          womb ovaries lights
she must be dying . . .
                         once
is all

this girl at school
it caught between her thighs
broken open she . . .
                    spilled
a sack of flour . . .
            so it was whispered

Mummy   Mom . . . Oh.
                    Mommy
                         she dreams her mother's
                    sewing place in the attic   knitting
                    the birthday night dress   ribbons   lace
                         cut & pinned   work table
                    as if its maker were coming back   so
                         she is not surprised to find
          her in faded blue jeans   woolly lime green top
                    against the window surrounded
                         by a wavering scent of Joy
          Mother reaches for bites of the sun   turning
                    gently in air she says   here
                         have a bit of real food

surely she walks streets parks
        her breasts aching at
            every small face
                wincing
          at every cry   every child
       crippled at church doors
years later   he searched for his
first *but could not find her*
among death & four
          thousand
unable to remember
her birth date
within two years

         meanwhile her bones hummed
            knowing

                  what will happen
                    defines
               what has happened
                    defines
                 what will happen
                    defines
        us rebellious tame confused

       daughters
   even in our secret spaces
     deep inside ourselves
       to every penis

      and ever so?

she looks over at me as if to say
to imagine is to act   end
this quickly   but i
have torn this
                    from winter
beneath the Rockies
she exists existed will exist in her terrible cocoon
and none of this is fairy tale

for some moments she swallows thickening
air then she understands
its water has broken
gingerly she drags herself up
floors tilt   walls
narrow & pulse around her
she pulls towels from racks

it comes
suddenly   after all
an awesome urge to evacuate
she stoops   begins to push   pushshshsh
pain shocks her   she is floating high
above the tub watching this squatting
fifteen year old noise in agony
horror   in a kind of disbelief
innocence torn away
as between her legs a baby's head appears
her body gives one final
jerk   one heaving push
it is thrust
from her in a welter of blood
muck   screaming

(they tell us we are what we eat
pretending an interest
in our health)
for millennia
we have swallowed
it all
seeking control we have swallowed
the woman's food
and we know the precise etiquette
the finding the secret buying the dawn waters
the pounding chopping bruising boiling burning   the pain
the fierce silence   the sleeping over or under despite
how tongue must curve
lips brush
how hard   how
soft the ball
what spices   herbs
bark   cactus   gums
plugs of crocodile
dung
of cotton soaked in
honey
of oils spiderwebs
at full moon
from dimmest
corners
such washes ash wine
vinegar lemon
to pills/foam/shields
such pain
daughter to
daughter

the girl leans back
pain ebbs   incredible
relief exhaustion washes
over   as she descends
rejoins the other

it is three o'clock

she falls asleep
refusing all
her legs open   *it* lies between
mottled   nasty   face down
squirming on cold enamel
breathing
. . . breathing

Mummy   Mom   Mummy

Happy Birthday Darling
pink candles   one big breath now
Happy Birthday to you-oo-ou

"Leave me . . . please . . . no please" her head burrows
into the rim of the world . . . Jenn? J? Jenn? JENN!
he has her by the shoulder   his face working . . . I
. . . I didn't know   look what you've done . . . a . . .
a baby fuck He's going to be furious He said I was
to check on you an' call him   what're we to do He'll
kill me! JENN? J?   a mild pang across her stomach
Josh wipes wipes his hands across the seat of his
pants   the way he always did before He dragged
him to the basement   "*It's* dead"   she says flatly   "*it*
must be nobody wants *it*"   *It* isn't!   tightened lips

this stone at centre

                          still wyfman owing windsucker welcome
if all fails   abandonment   suffocation   exposure

church   · law   custom

                                          wyman
                        what is
to be done
besides
                                       a poem
in broad brush strokes
                                       fashioned
(note the shading of space
midnight sparkle
the brown water Os   *in*
certain pieties

besides   *compliance*
a march   placards   chain
to bind ourselves   *to*
                                      a world
whose precise terms
wandering from night window
to night window
remain always the same
while we dangle after
                                    a definition
theirs

eyes search clocks   remember Father   she screams
"CUT *IT* OFF!"   OK OK   Josh searches   nail scissors
looks at the dead purple thing joining his sister to
her baby   Should I get hot water   they look at each
other   "It said in the book you knot it at both ends
wash the scissors"   he kneels trying not to look   Will
it hurt   *"It's* dead"   he swings away violently sick   she
throws a towel over herself quickly   "What time is it?"
Nearly four   they fumble together   the baby squalls
squalls   their eyes meet   Can't you feed *it*   she draws
back into herself   "No No No No"   there is this
bloody mess   she sits a long time   cramps afterbirth
bleeding He'll smell . . .   faint   fearful she Lysols tub
wall floor hangs new towels   five-twenty   she can hear
it   she makes a bundle of towels rags   leans her way to
her room   thin insistent squalling again   Josh wraps
the baby intently   old blue blanket she's used for
Boogie Bear   he lines the box with newspapers
suggests she fold towels   says   gruff If He finds out
He'll kill us   Mrs. Jameson loves kids   let's give *it* to
her   startled pleased she begins to cry   "Josh that's
great! really rad!"   Oh shut up   this room stinks   I'll
take *it* now   "Think *it's* warm enough?"   she stares at
the tiny red face   "I'd better feed her"   she pushes her nipple
into its lips squeezes as she has seen in films   baby
doesn't know how either   creamish stuff trickles from
its mouth   *it* pulls on her breast   squalls   You're not
doing it right   hurry   He'll be home   "Okay Josh OK"
she cuddles the warm body   solid like Boogie Bear but
squirming   "She has my eyes

and lonely for each other
caught in this
dance of ancestral design
forever in the ring
of their fires their fears
their primeval night lapping
careful of the circle
we weave in and out of
their drumming   their call
and response   the piercing
threnody of our mothers
each shuffle   each swaying
body shaping shaping   we carry
earth   arms heads all true to their
terrible instinct
their grammar of the sexes
whatever the age demands
knowing the blood rush knowing pain bloodrush
searing mutilation soul-pain bloodrush fear pain

knowing too   women do not howl it annoys it angers
it's impolite/impolitic

his/her: determiner — also indicates ownership if perceived
as pronoun
main/significant: adjective — in English between the determiner
and its noun only an adjective and its intensifier may
be placed; also implies others less significant
squeeze/other: noun — a different part of the universe of being;
the act of pressing the juice out of something; usually
the object is discarded after its usefulness has
evaporated

Put more towels on   it's cold   think they'll hear
her?"   *It's* your baby   she feels sick   wraps Bear's
diaper between tiny legs   that other mouth   no
no daughter should go naked

from halfway down
the stairs   she watches him
carry her burden out   relief
lifts her   she is swirling round
and round in a high place
full of white birds
their thin cries
without threat   wings brush her
face   flutter in her tummy

she hears the door slam shut
smiles   it is only Josh

because we believe in en(dis)abling difference
in the secret heart we believe
at coiled root we believe
we believe it a matter of science
we think it a matter of truth
if we do not build on "fact" what is
shelter except "faith" but
science constructs a fiction   religion
a myth   then hastens to strengthen
shoring up walls of words   finding
bedrock   raising columns to legitimize
to rationalize the political
under such roofs we empty goblets of metaphor
suck the marrow of image
and they become   and bone
of our bone   they speak us
run wild in our stories   structure
our making   our dreams
incorrigible
our texts   our games   our lives
because we fear the desert   its loneliness
because we do not know how to start over
lay foundations   neuter old metaphor
dream new dreams
how to see through   see
beyond screens of culture/gender/race
to persons   I write
for us all   we must change
the fictions before the fictions
play us out   their unsubtle denouements
skies without cloud
earth without rivers or smiles